Content

FIND 6 DIFFERENCES

FIND 7 DIFFERENCES

FIND 7 DIFFERENCES

FIND 7 DIFFERENCES

FIND 7 DIFFERENCES

FIND 10 DIFFERENCES

FIND 6 DIFFERENCES

FIND 6 DIFFERENCES

FIND 6 DIFFERENCES

FIND 6 DIFFERENCES

FIND 6 DIFFERENCES

FIND 7 DIFFERENCES

FIND 7 DIFFERENCES

FIND 7 DIFFERENCES

FIND 7 DIFFERENCES

FIND 7 DIFFERENCES

FIND 7 DIFFERENCES

FIND 7 DIFFERENCES

FIND 7 DIFFERENCES

FIND 7 DIFFERENCES

FIND 7 DIFFERENCES

FIND 7 DIFFERENCES

FIND 7 DIFFERENCES

FIND 7 DIFFERENCES

FIND 7 DIFFERENCES

FIND 7 DIFFERENCES

FIND 7 DIFFERENCES

FIND 7 DIFFERENCES

FIND 7 DIFFERENCES

FIND 10 DIFFERENCES

FIND 10 DIFFERENCES

FIND 10 DIFFERENCES

FIND 10 DIFFERENCES

FIND 10 DIFFERENCES

FIND 10 DIFFERENCES

FIND 10 DIFFERENCES

FIND 10 DIFFERENCES

FIND 10 DIFFERENCES

FIND 10 DIFFERENCES

Answers

Answers

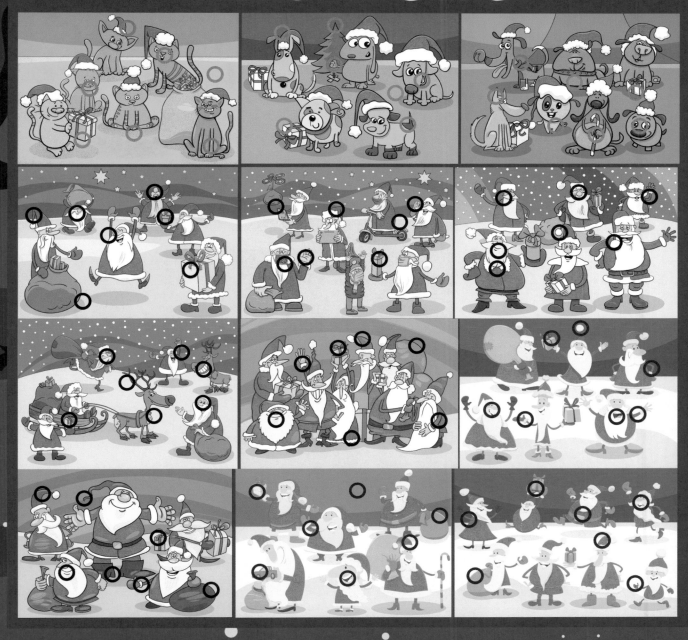

Answers

One last thing...

We would love to hear your comments about this book.

If you liked this book or found it helpful, we would appreciate it if you would post a short review on Amazon. Your support makes all the difference and we personally read all reviews.

If you would like to leave a review, just click on the review link on the Amazon page for this book.

We thank you for your support.

Made in the USA
Columbia, SC
24 November 2023

26948703R00022